Trees Count

Trish Holland

Teaching Strategies • Washington D.C.

For Teaching Strategies, Inc.
Publisher: Larry Bram
Editorial Director: Hilary Parrish Nelson
VP Curriculum and Assessment: Cate Heroman
Product Manager: Kai-leé Berke
Book Development Team: Sherrie Rudick and Jan Greenberg
Project Manager: Jo A. Wilson

For Q2AMedia
Editorial Director: Bonnie Dobkin
Editor and Curriculum Adviser: Suzanne Barchers
Program Manager: Gayatri Singh
Creative Director: Simmi Sikka
Project Manager: Santosh Vasudevan
Designer: Dalbir Singh
Picture Researchers: Judy Brown & Anita Gill

Picture Credits
t-top b-bottom c-center l-left r-right

Cover: Jim Barber/Shutterstock, Shutterstock, Yasonya/Dreamstime, Laura Gangi Pond/Bigstockphoto, Tono Balaguer/Shutterstock, Marilyn Barbone/Shutterstock, Le Do/Shutterstock, Bronwyn Photo/Shutterstock, Zentilia/123RF, Newton Page/Istockphoto.

Back Cover: Liviu Toader/Shutterstock.

Title Page: Jim Barber/Shutterstock, Shutterstock, Yasonya/Dreamstime, Laura Gangi Pond/Bigstockphoto, Tono Balaguer/Shutterstock, Marilyn Barbone/Shutterstock, Le Do/Shutterstock, Bronwyn Photo/Shutterstock, Zentilia/123RF, Newton Page/Istockphoto.

Insides: Marilyna Barbone/Dreamtime: 3, Tiffany Orpana/Istockphoto: 4t, Anette Linnea Rasmussen/Dreamstime: 4b, Ralphele/Fotolia: 5t, Penny Medders/123RF: 5b, Therese McKeon/Istockphoto: 6l, Rick Wylie/Istockphoto, Tim Pleasant/Shutterstock: 6r, Laurin Rinder/Fotolia: 7l, Pond Shots/Bigstockphoto: 7r, Graham S.klotz/Shutterstock: 8t, Aimin Tang/Istockphoto: 8b, Richard Mcguirk/Dreamstime: 9l, Macka/Shutterstock, Shutterstock: 9r, ZMUPicture/Shutterstock: 10t, Ralf Siegele/Istockphoto: 10b, Dreamstime: 11l, Jozsef Szasz – Fabian/Dreamstime: 11r, Kathryn Bell/Shutterstock, Xin Guo/Dreamstime: 12t, Bonnie Watton/Shutterstock: 12b, Sergey Galushko/Dreamstime: 13t, Bronwyn Photo/Serg64/Shutterstock: 13b, 24, Shutterstock: 14t, Ralf Siegele/Istockphoto: 14b, Yasonya/Dreamstime: 15t, Elena Elisseeva/Shutterstock: 15b, 24, Liviu Toader/Shutterstock: 16t, Newton Page/Istockphoto: 16b, 24, Pond Shots/Bigstockphoto: 17t, Lane Erickson/123RF: 17b, 24, Rick Wylie/Istockphoto, Tim Pleasant/Shutterstock: 18t, Zentilia/123RF: 18b, 24, Tono Balaguer/Shutterstock: 19t, Julija Sapic/Shutterstock: 19b, Istockphoto: 20t, Anette Linnea Rasmussen/Dreamstime: 20c, Jan Martin Will/Dreamstime: 20b, 24, Istockphoto: 21t, Marilyn Barbone/Shutterstock: 21b, 24, Jim Barber/Shutterstock: 22, Brozova/Fotolia: 23, Lane Erickson/123RF, Jan Martin Will/Shutterstock, Bronwyn Photo/Shutterstock, 123rf, Marilyn Barbone/Shutterstock, Jan Martin Will/Dreamstime, Newton Page/Istockphoto, Le Do/Shutterstock, Elena Elisseeva/Shutterstock, Julija Sapic/Shutterstock: 24.

Teaching Strategies, Inc.
P.O. Box 42243
Washington, DC 20015
www.TeachingStrategies.com

ISBN: 978-1-60617-128-8

Library of Congress Cataloging-in-Publication Data
Holland, Trish.
  Trees count / Trish Holland.
    p. cm.
  ISBN 978-1-60617-128-8
  1. Counting—Juvenile literature. 2. Trees—Juvenile literature. I. Title.
  QA113.H66 2010
  513.2'11—dc22
                            2009044304
CPSIA tracking label information:
RR Donnelley, Shenzhen, China
Date of Production: June 2014
Cohort: Batch 3

Printed and bound in China

5 6 7 8 9 10	15 14
Printing	Year Printed

1 Trunk

I am an OAK tree,
Strong enough for fun.
I can hold your treehouse.
Count my trunk — **ONE**.

2 Seeds

I am a MAPLE tree.
Seeds swirl down on you.
Watch them spinning as they fall.
Count the seeds — **TWO**.

3 Pecans

I am a PECAN tree.
You can swing from me.
Open up these fresh pecans.
Count them now — **THREE**.

4 Knotholes

I am an ELM tree.
Squirrels and birds galore
Build their homes inside me.
Count my knotholes — **FOUR**.

5 Leaves

I am an ASPEN tree.
Fall brings me alive.
Heart-shaped leaves turn golden.
Count my leaves — **FIVE**.

6 Buds

I am a DOGWOOD tree.
In winter, I'm just sticks.
Blossoms burst in springtime.
Count my buds — **SIX**.

7 Cones

I am a PINE tree,
Stretching to the heavens.
Pick a pile of pine cones.
Count them now — **SEVEN**.

8 Apples

I am an APPLE tree.
You won't want to wait.
Munch and crunch my tasty fruit.
Count my apples — **EIGHT**.

9 Nuts

I am a WALNUT tree.
Would you like to dine?
Crack my shells wide open.
Count the nuts — **NINE**.

10 Flowers

I am a MAGNOLIA tree,
Growing in a glen
With blooms as big as pie plates.
Count my flowers — **TEN**.

I am the WALNUT tree.
Walnuts taste so fine.
As you nibbled on them,
Did you count **NINE**?

I am the APPLE tree.
Knew you couldn't wait!
When you ate my apples,
Did you count **EIGHT**?

I am the PINE tree,
Reaching for the heavens.
Picking prickly pine cones,
Did you count **SEVEN**?

I am the DOGWOOD tree,
Much more now than sticks.
Buds turned into flowers.
Can you count **SIX**?

I am the ASPEN tree.
In mountains where I thrive,
All my leaves are shimmering.
Did you count **FIVE**?

I am the ELM tree.
Critters, bugs, and more
Crawl inside my knotholes.
Do you count **FOUR**?

I am the PECAN tree,
Sturdy as can be.
As you crunched the tasty nuts,
Did you count **THREE**?

I am the MAPLE tree.
My seeds spun and flew.
Now they lie around my roots.
Did you count **TWO**?

I am the OAK tree,
Soaking up the sun.
When you climbed way up my trunk,
Did you count **ONE**?

Many Rings

I am an old tree.
I've seen many springs.
Someday I'll be **100**.
Can you count my rings?

1,000,000 Seeds

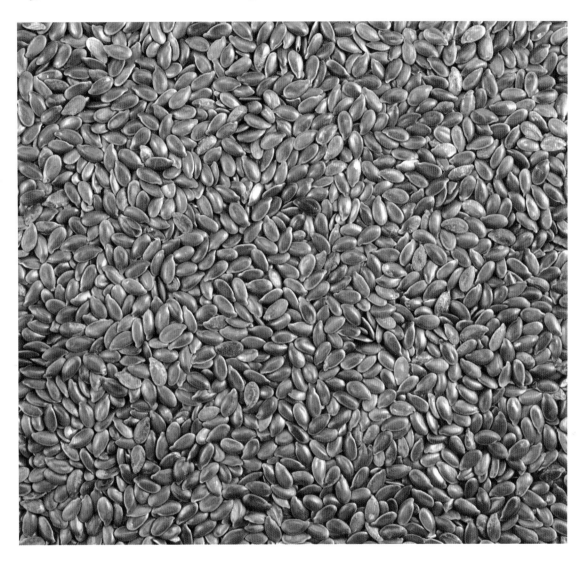

Every tree grows from a seed,
And here's a huge amount.
There could be a **MILLION**.
That's more than we can count!

10 Trees

We are all the trees you've met,
And we are so impressed.
You can count to **TEN** and back.
At counting, you're the best!